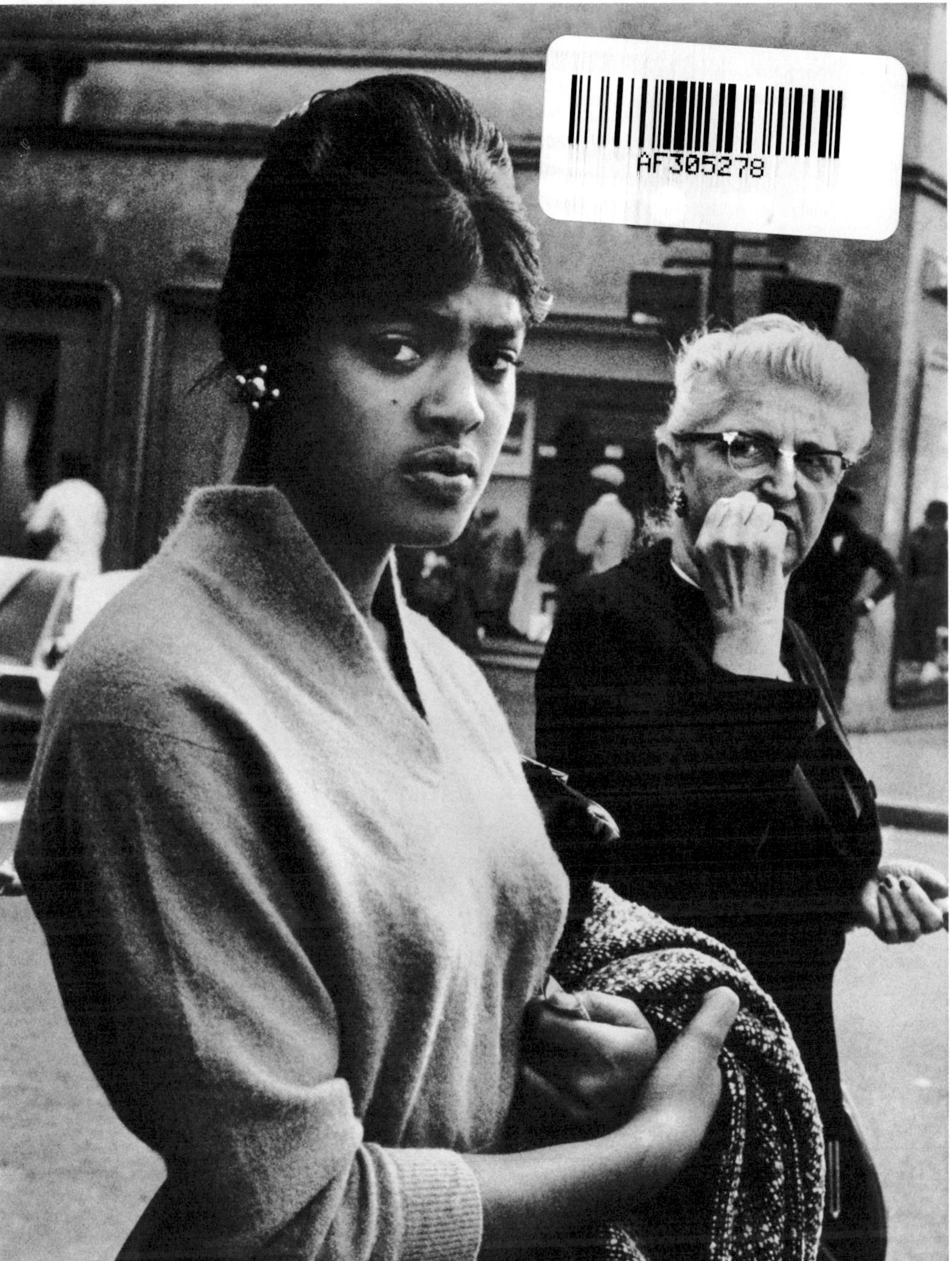

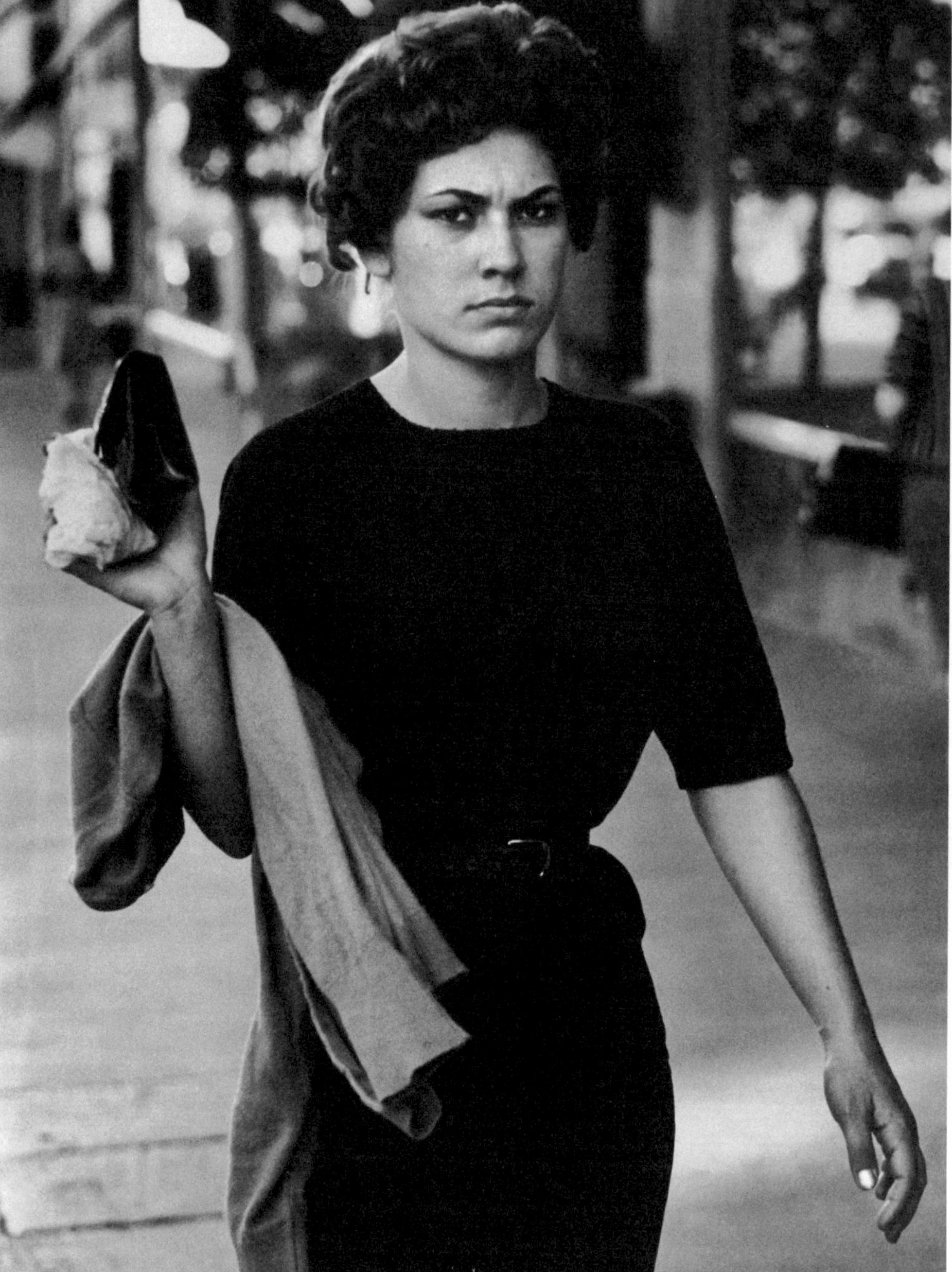

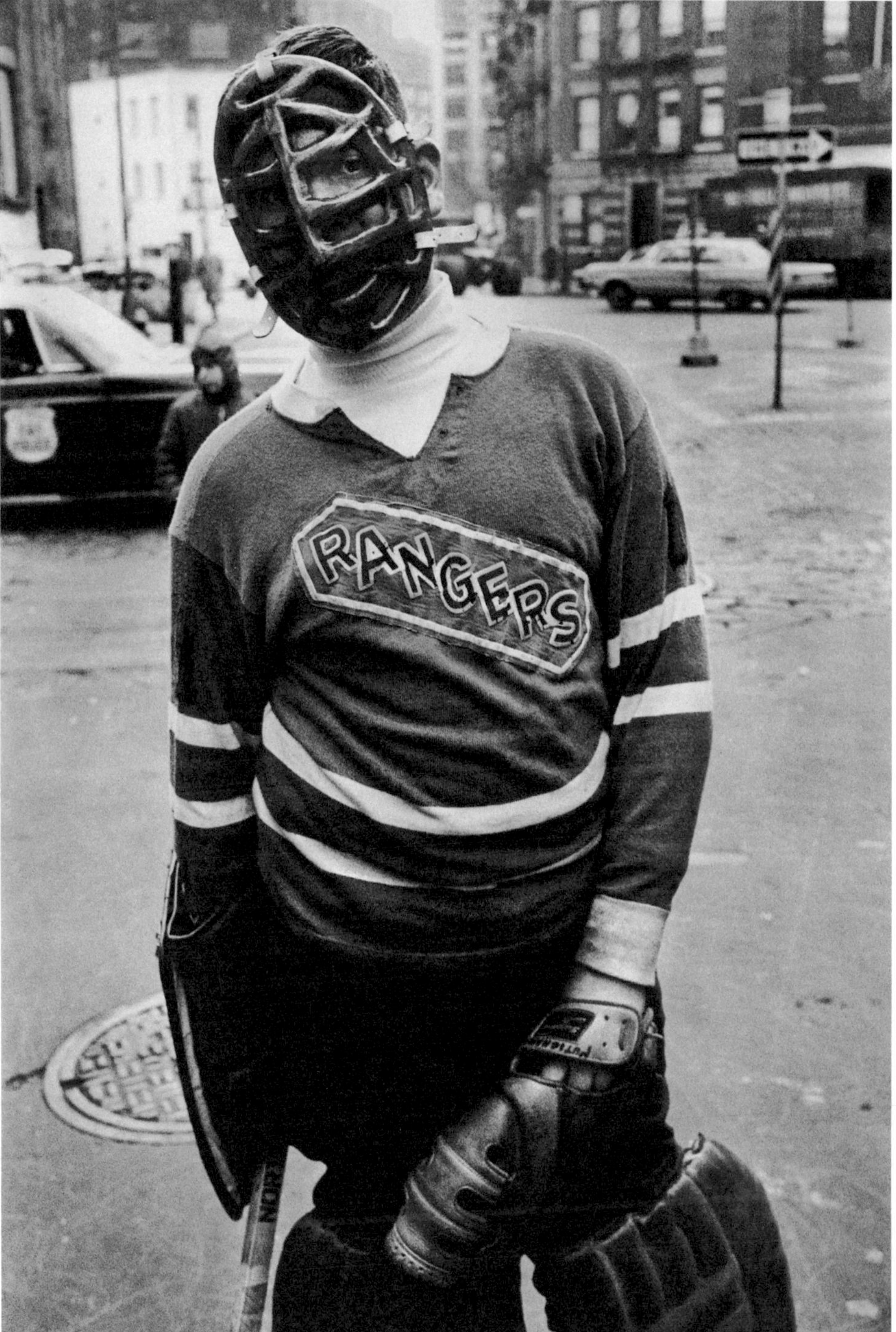

RANGERS

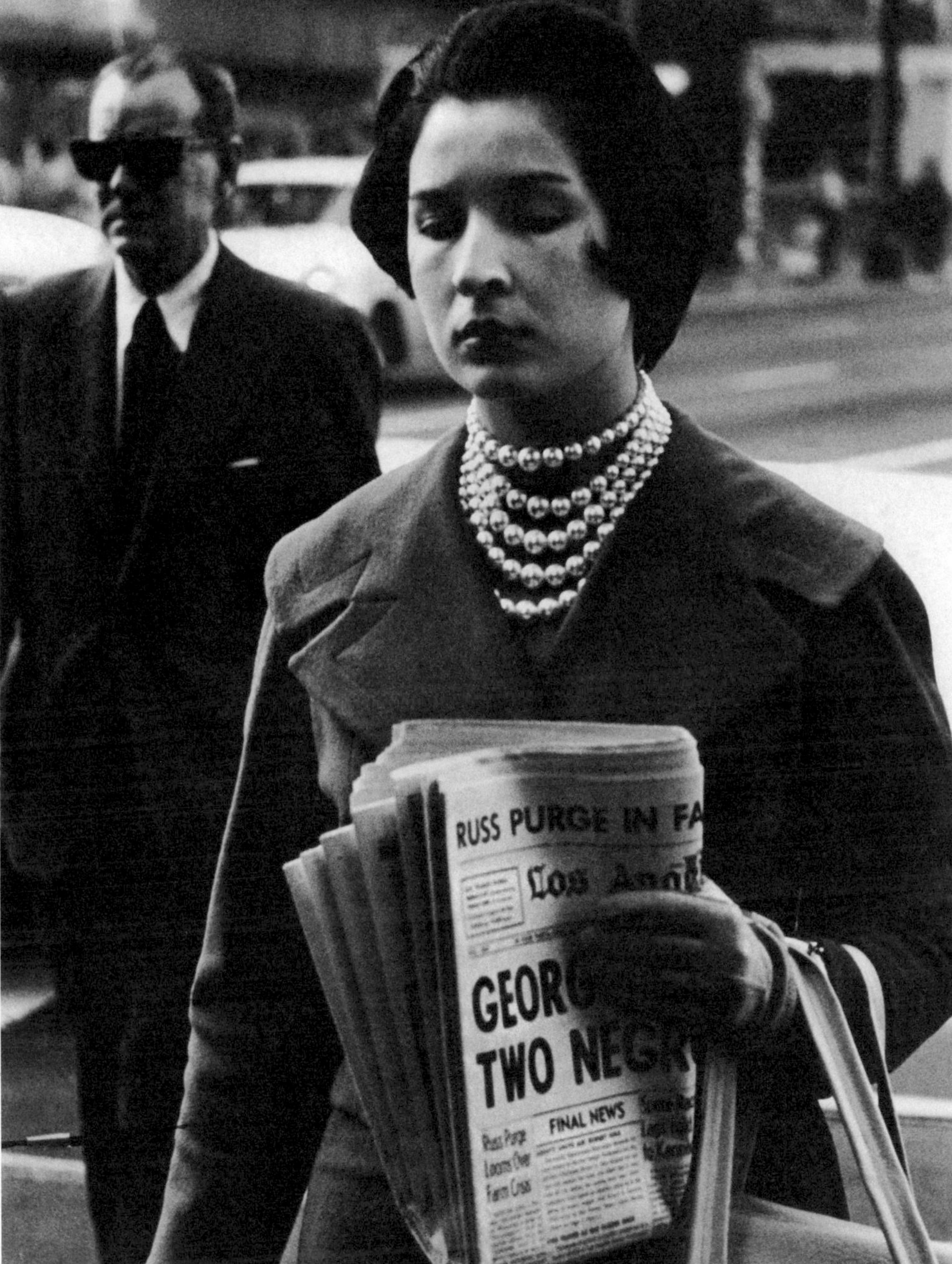

RUSS PURGE IN FA
Los Ang
GEORG
TWO NEGR
FINAL NEWS
Russ Purge
Locusts Over
Farm Crisis

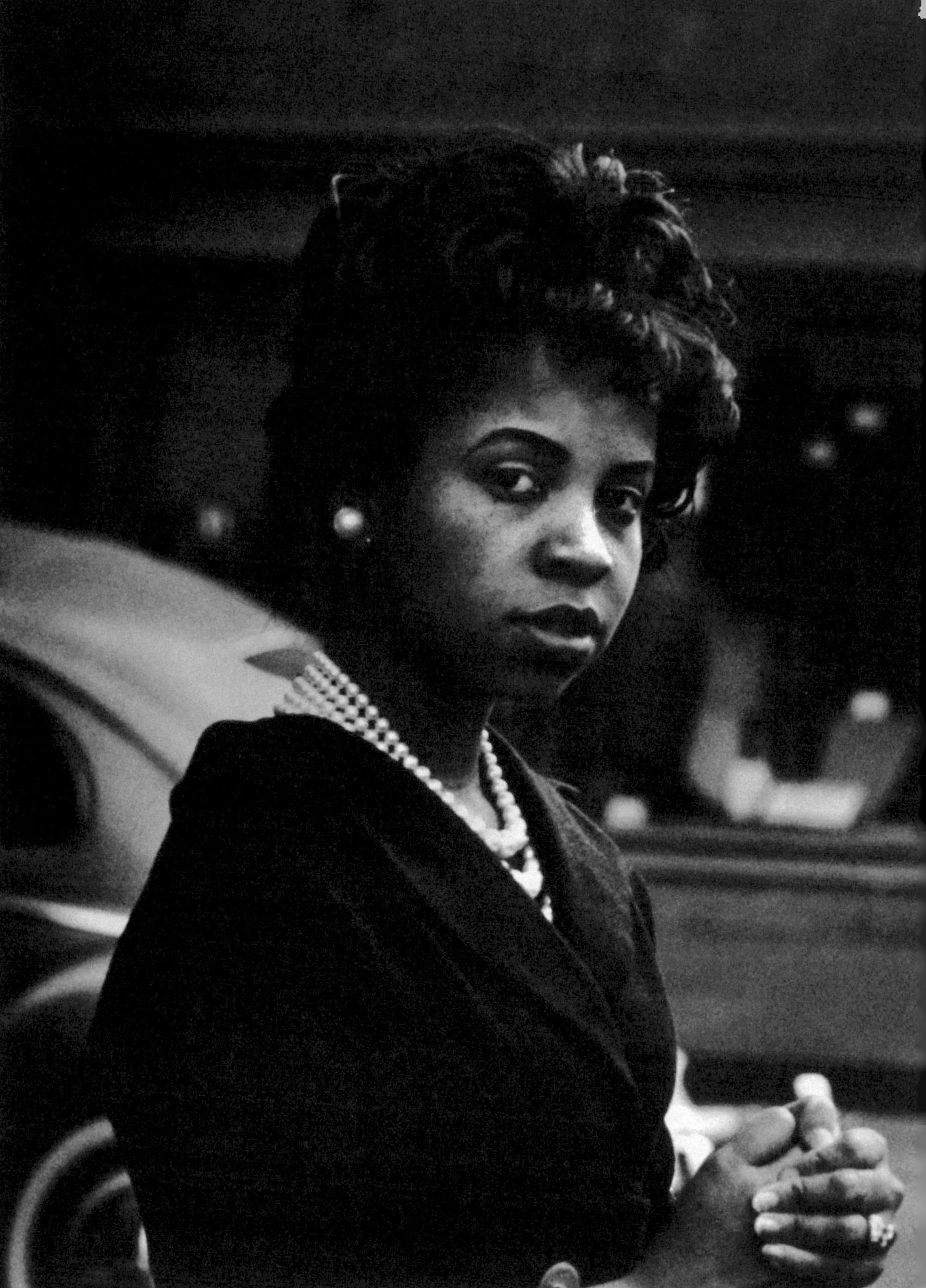

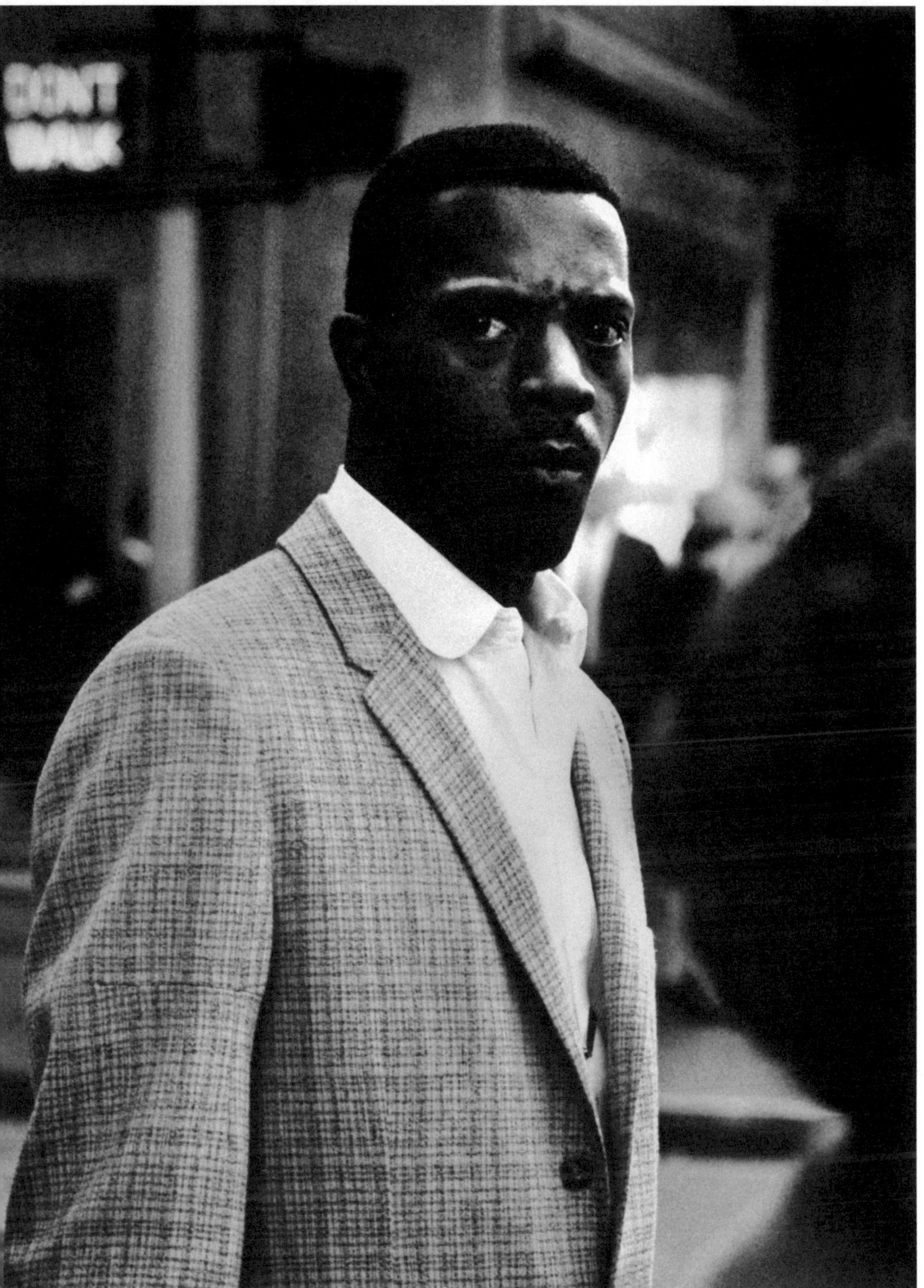

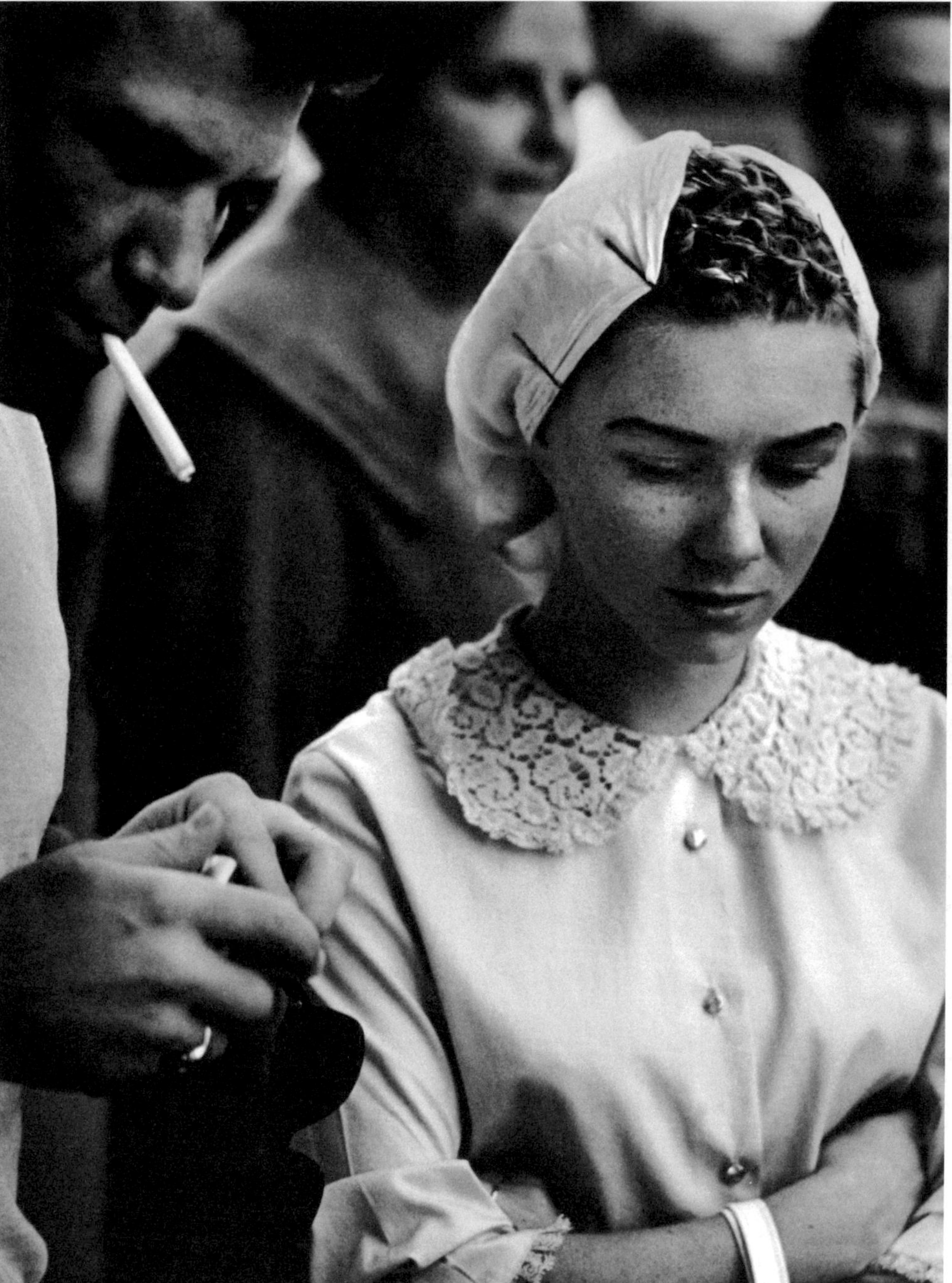

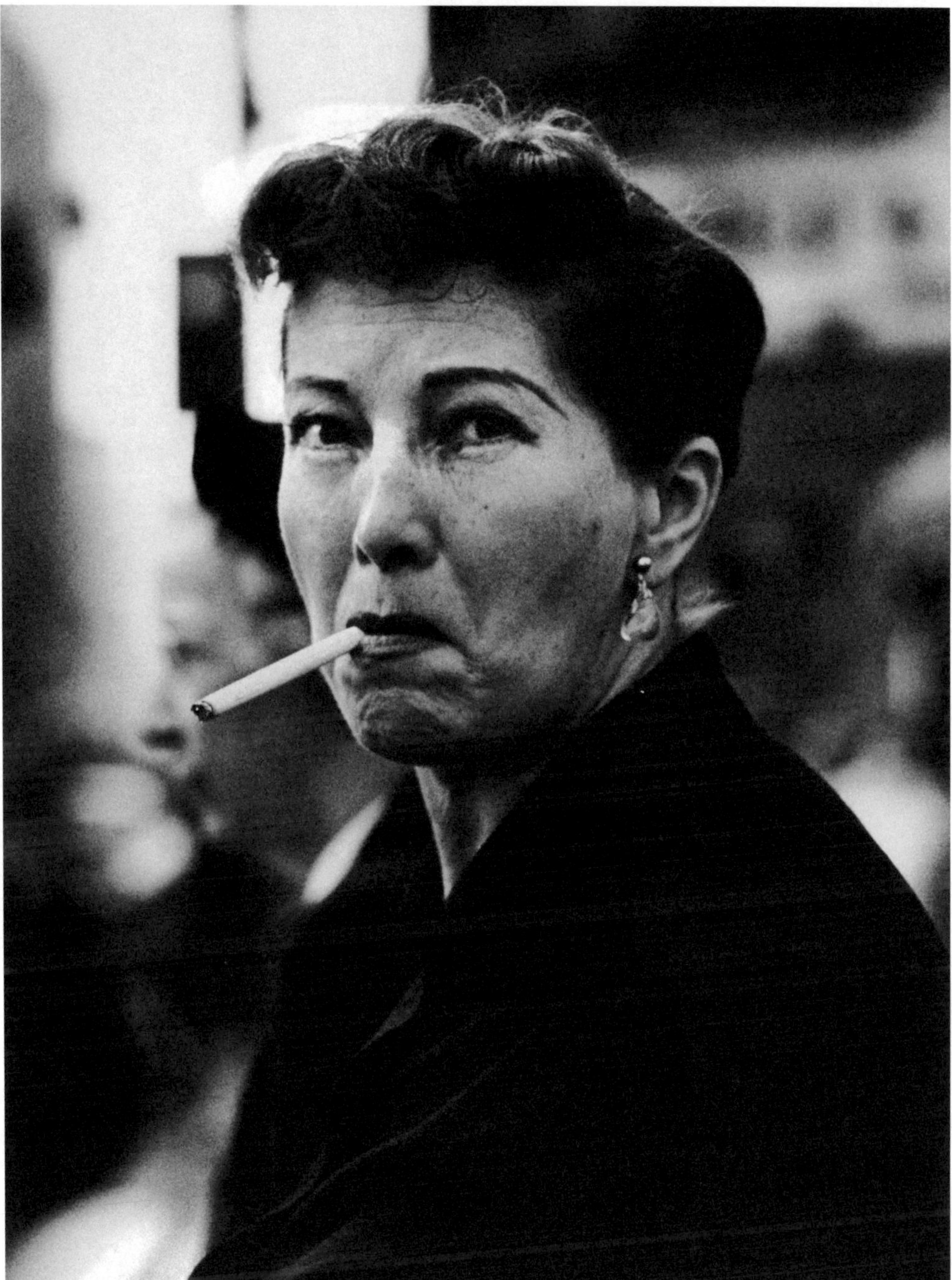

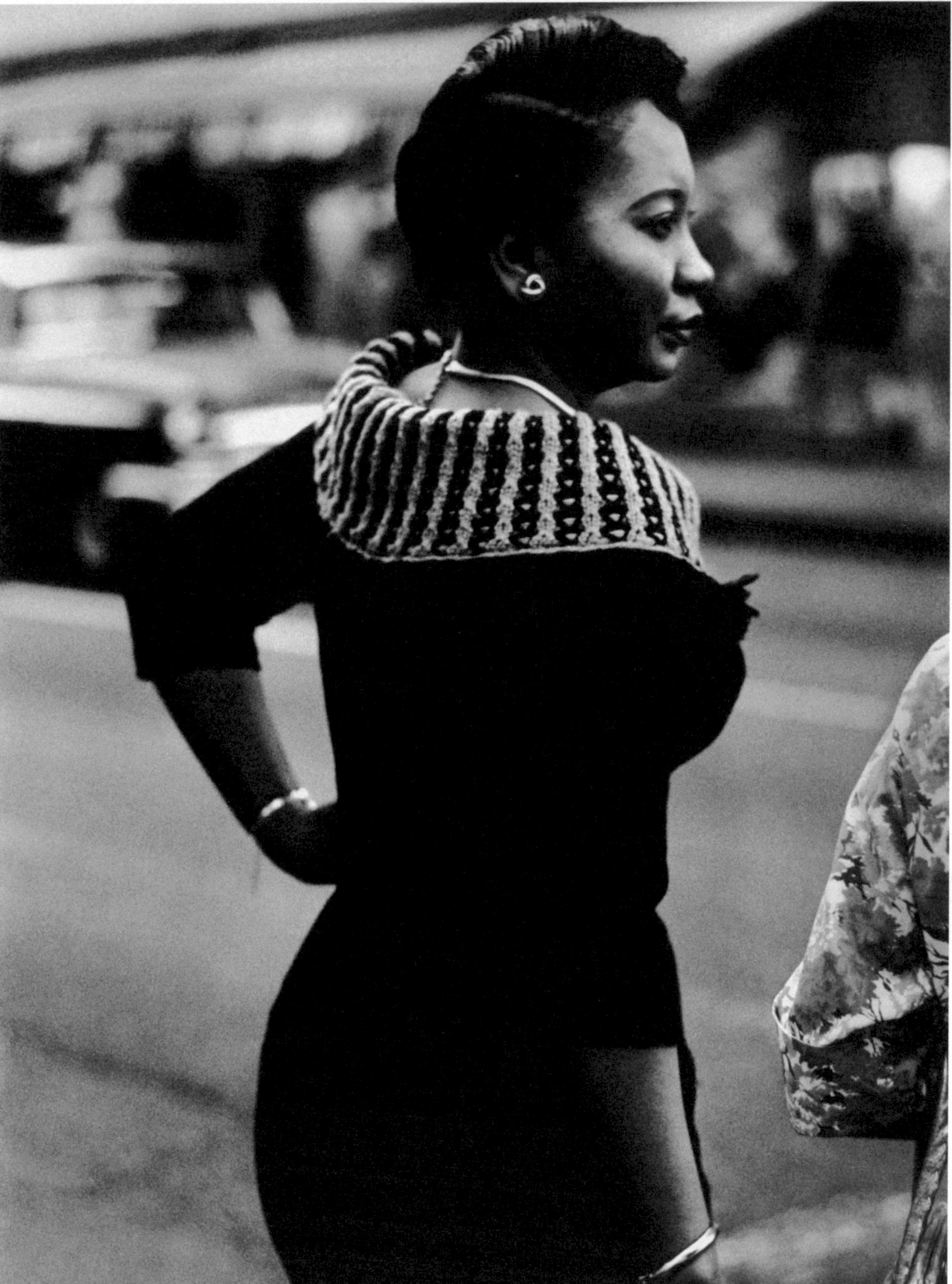

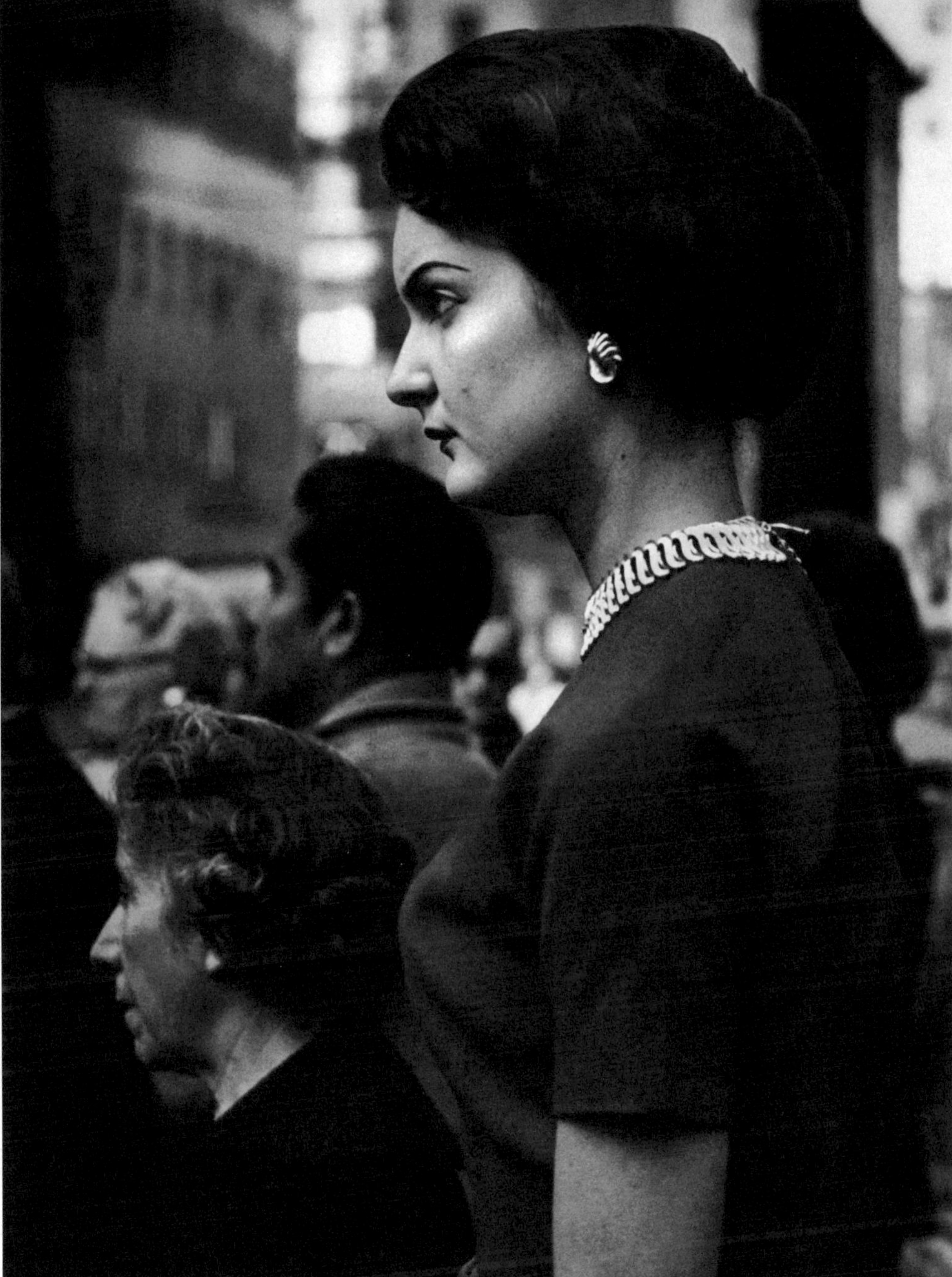

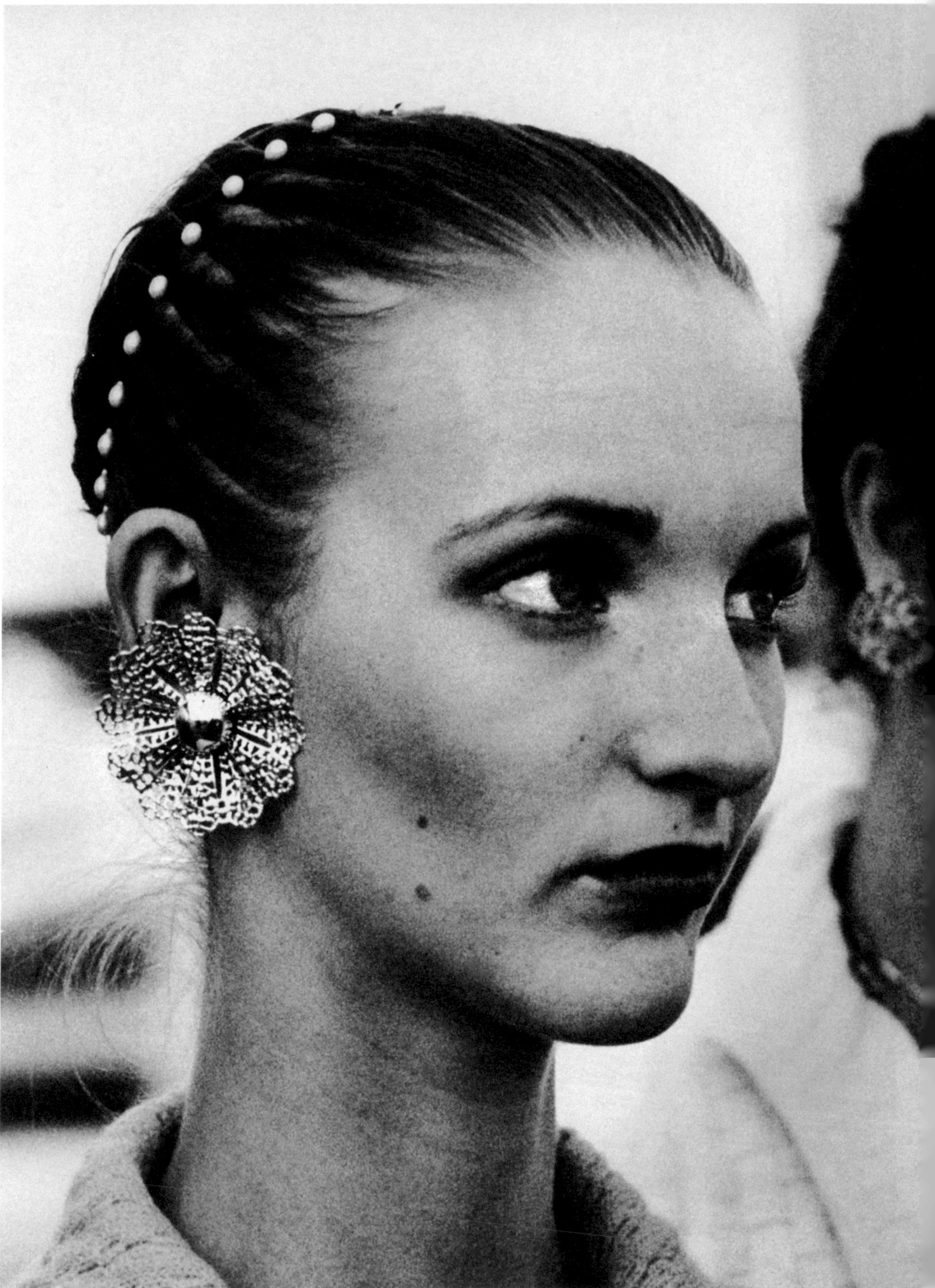

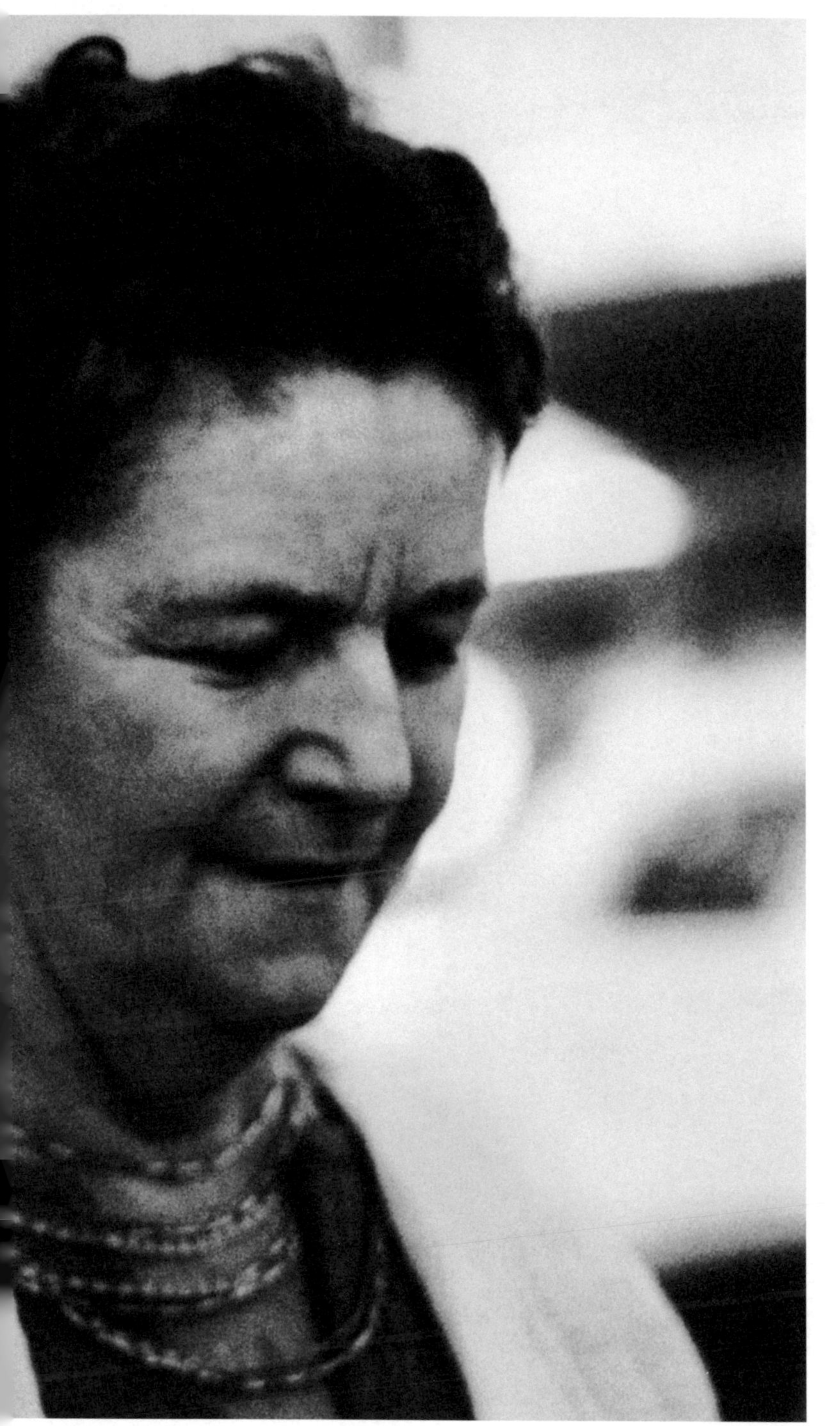

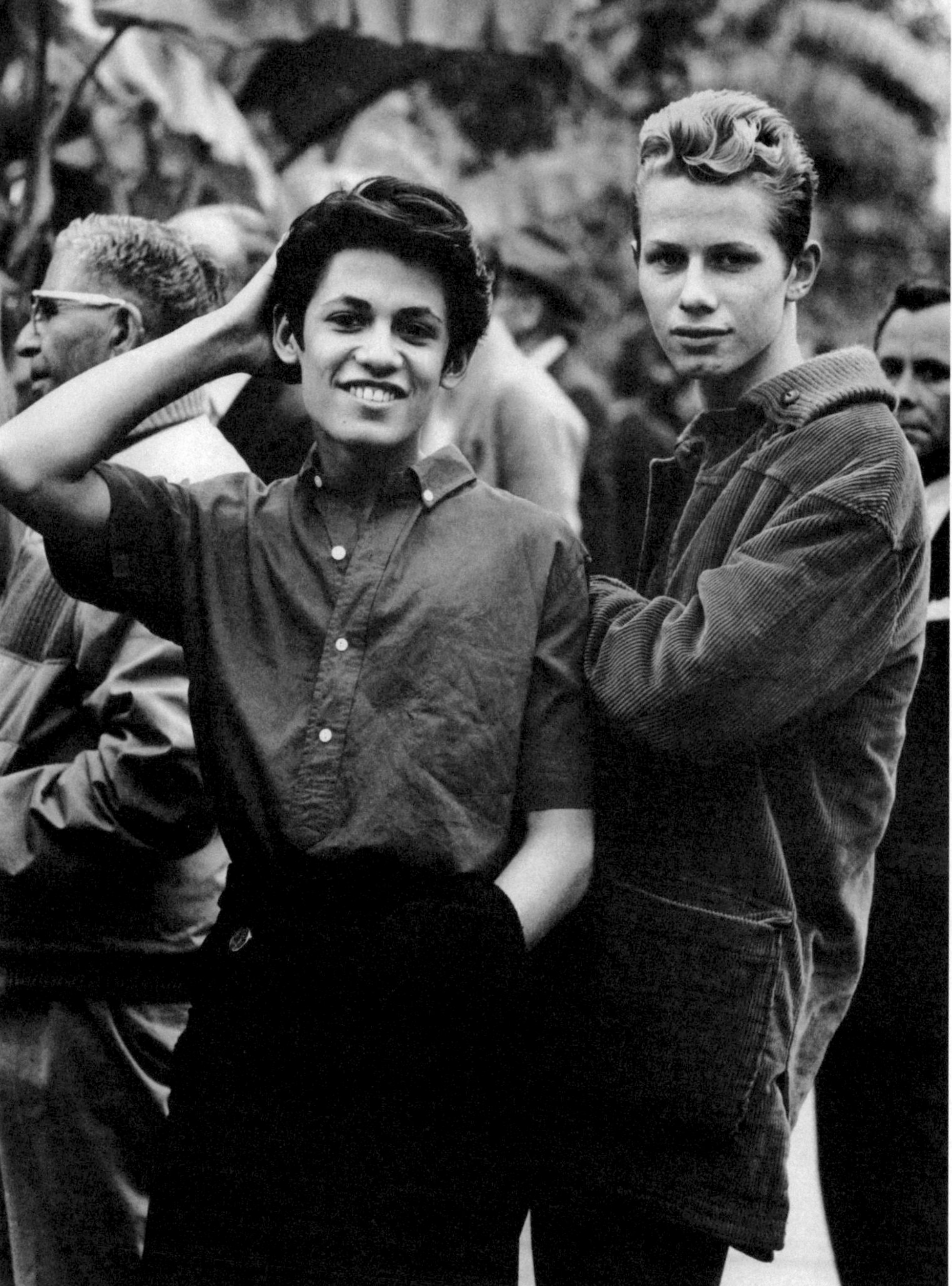

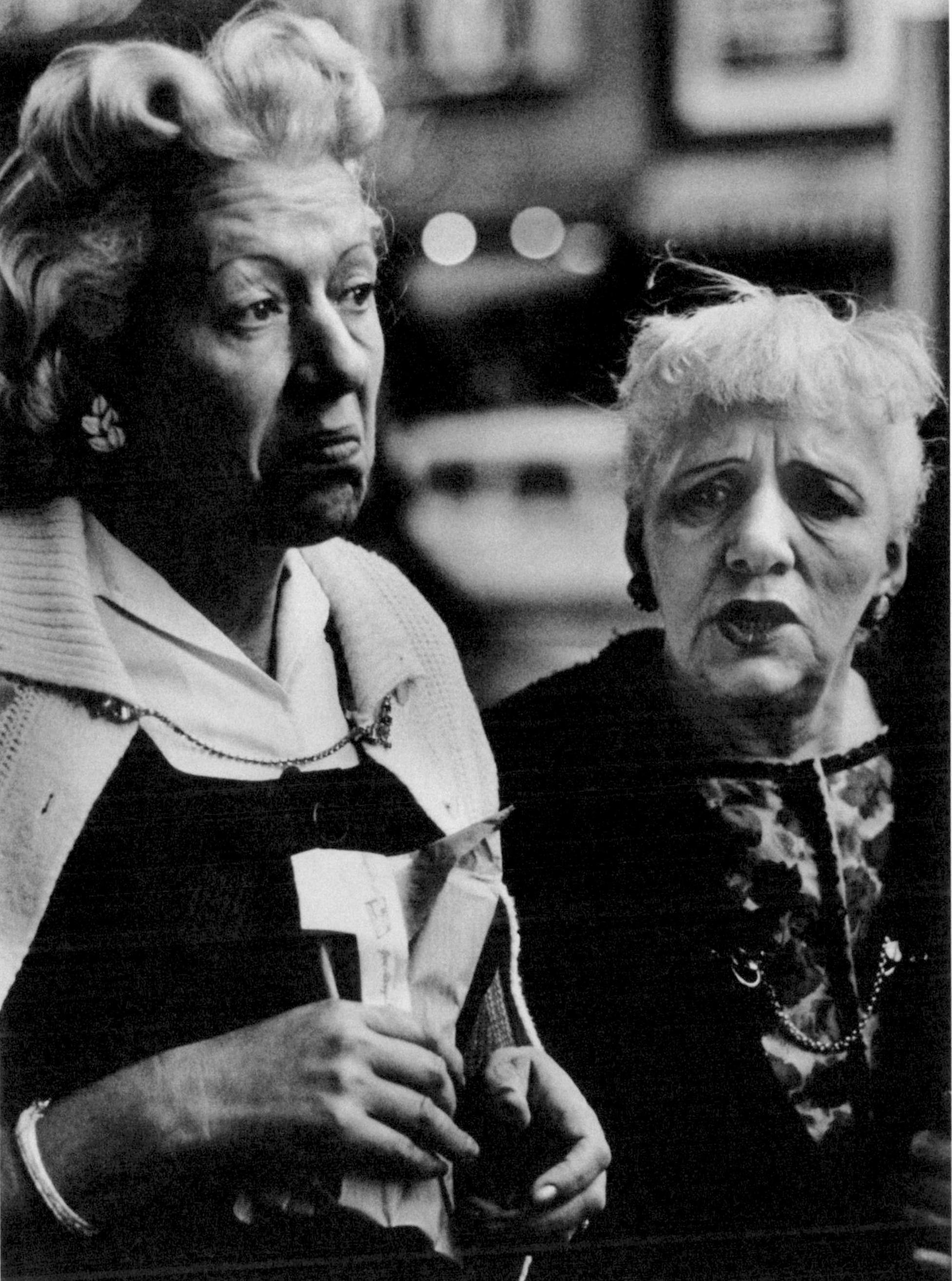

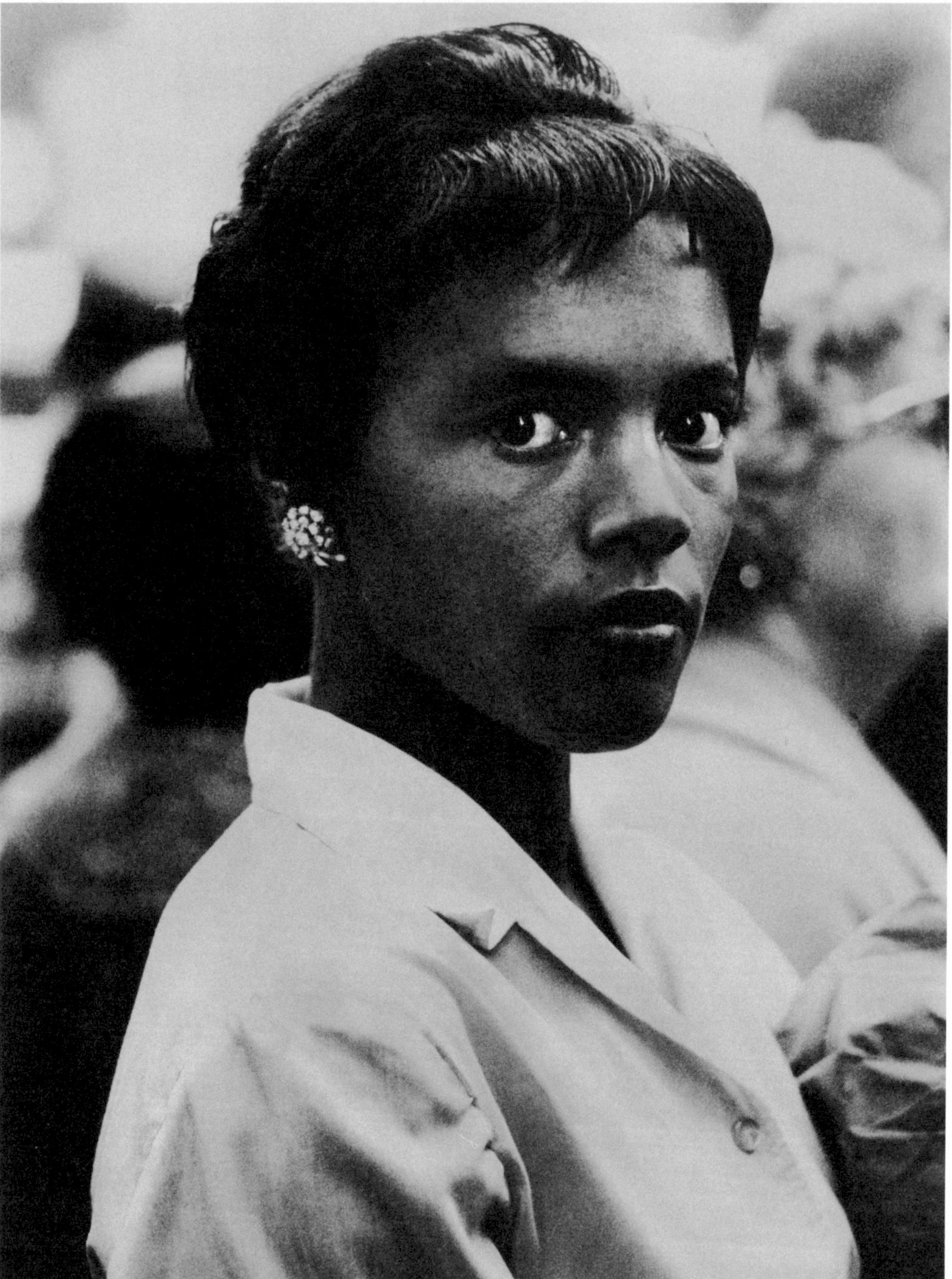

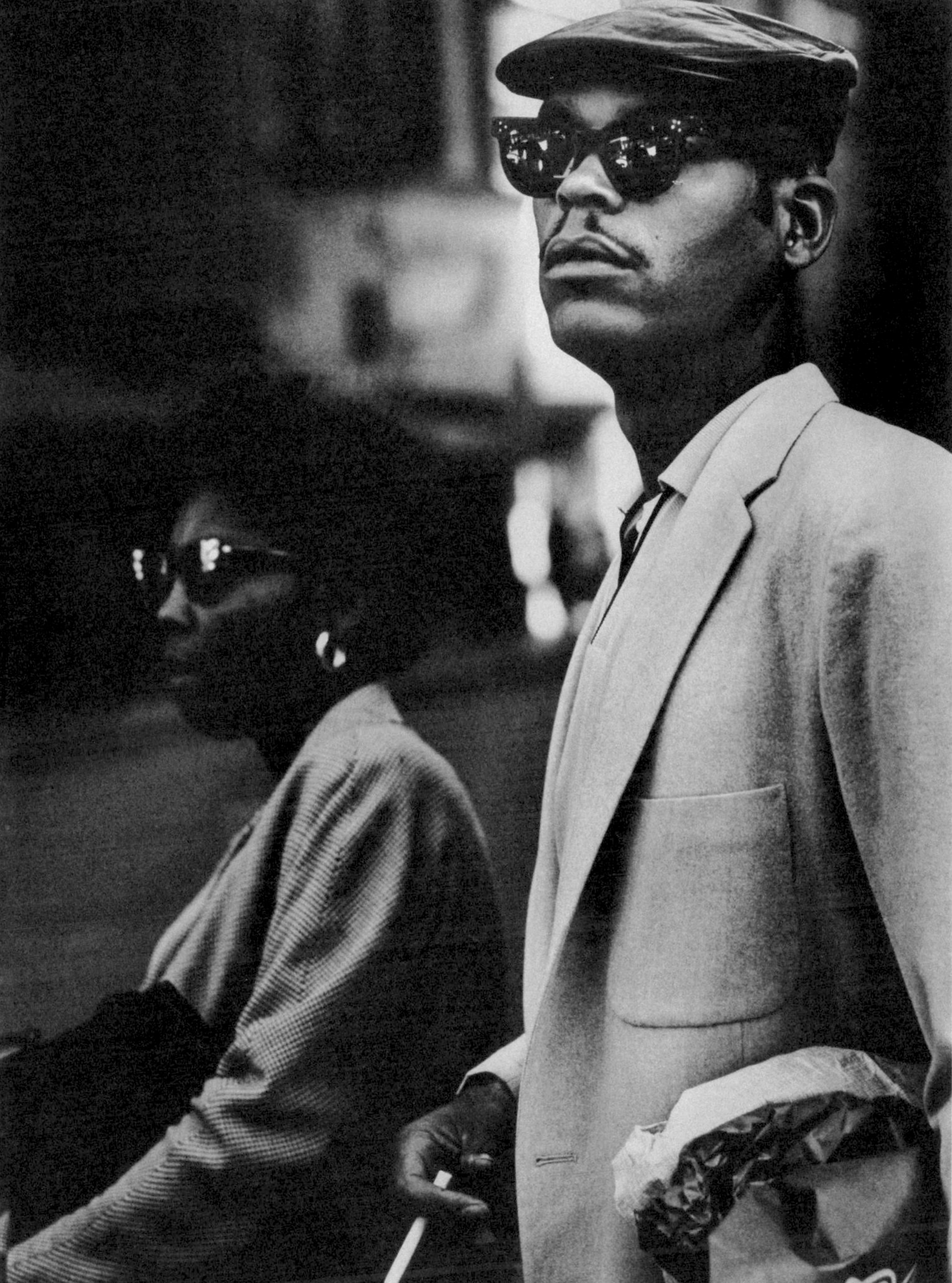

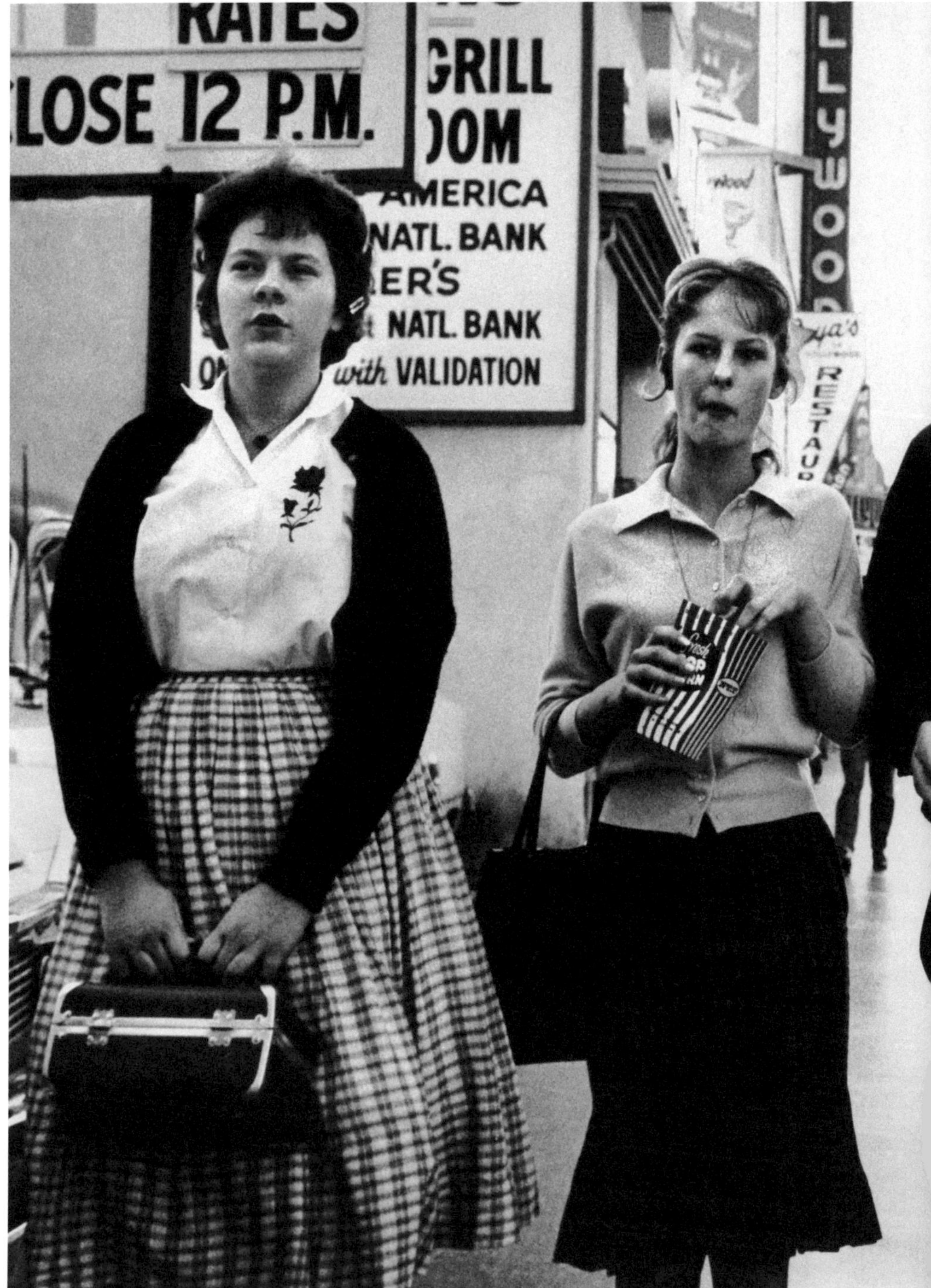

RATES
CLOSE 12 P.M.
GRILL
OOM
AMERICA
NATL. BANK
ER'S
NATL. BANK
with VALIDATION
RESTAUR

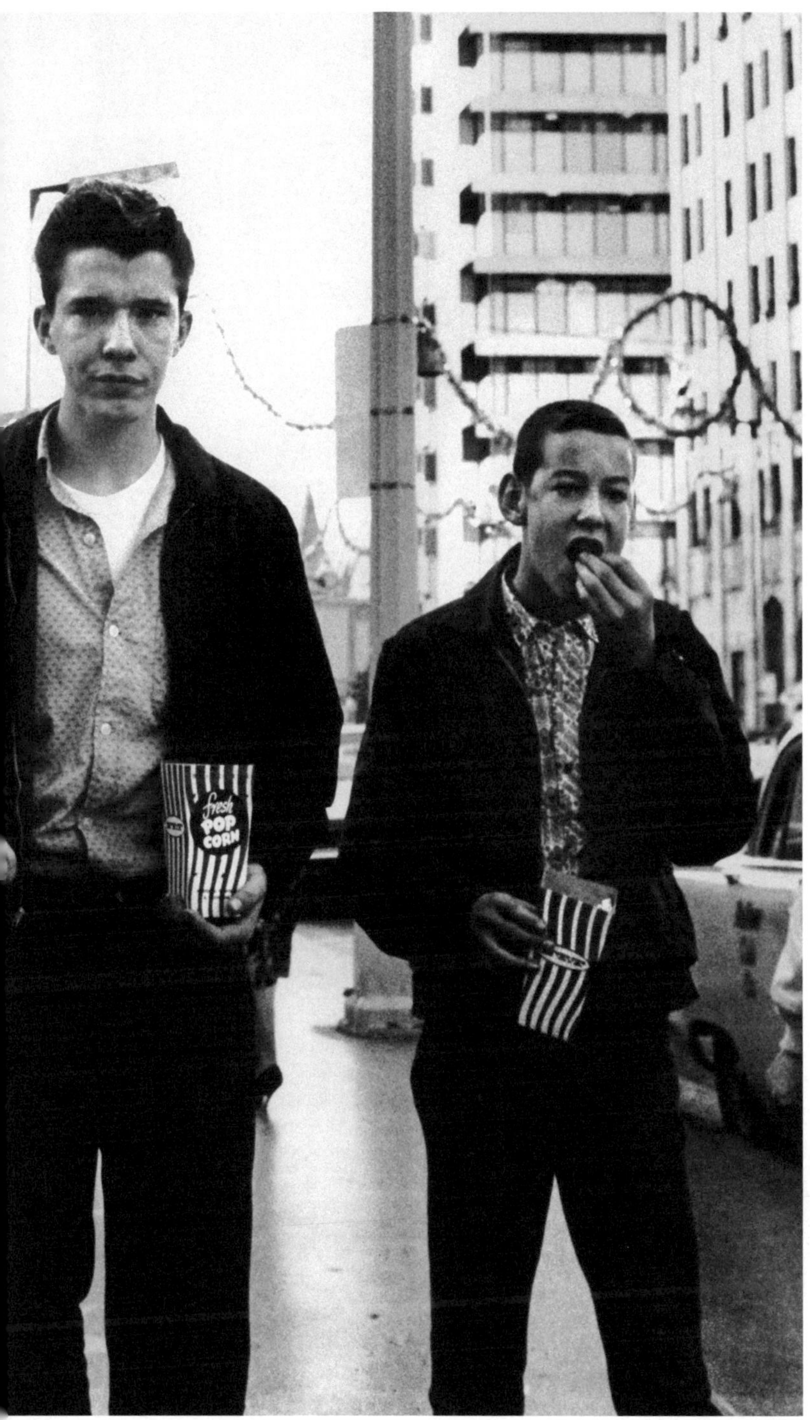

fresh
POP
CORN

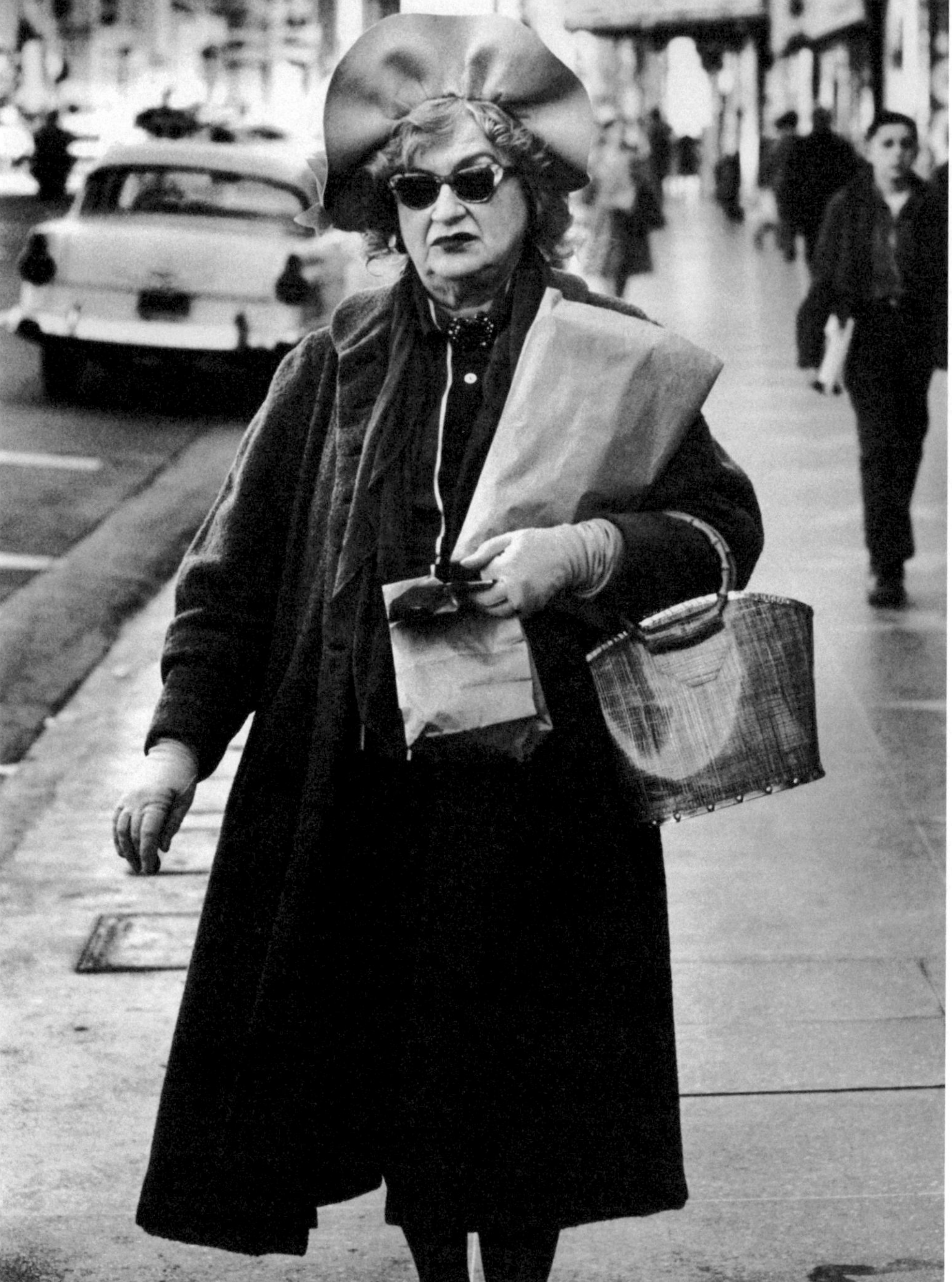

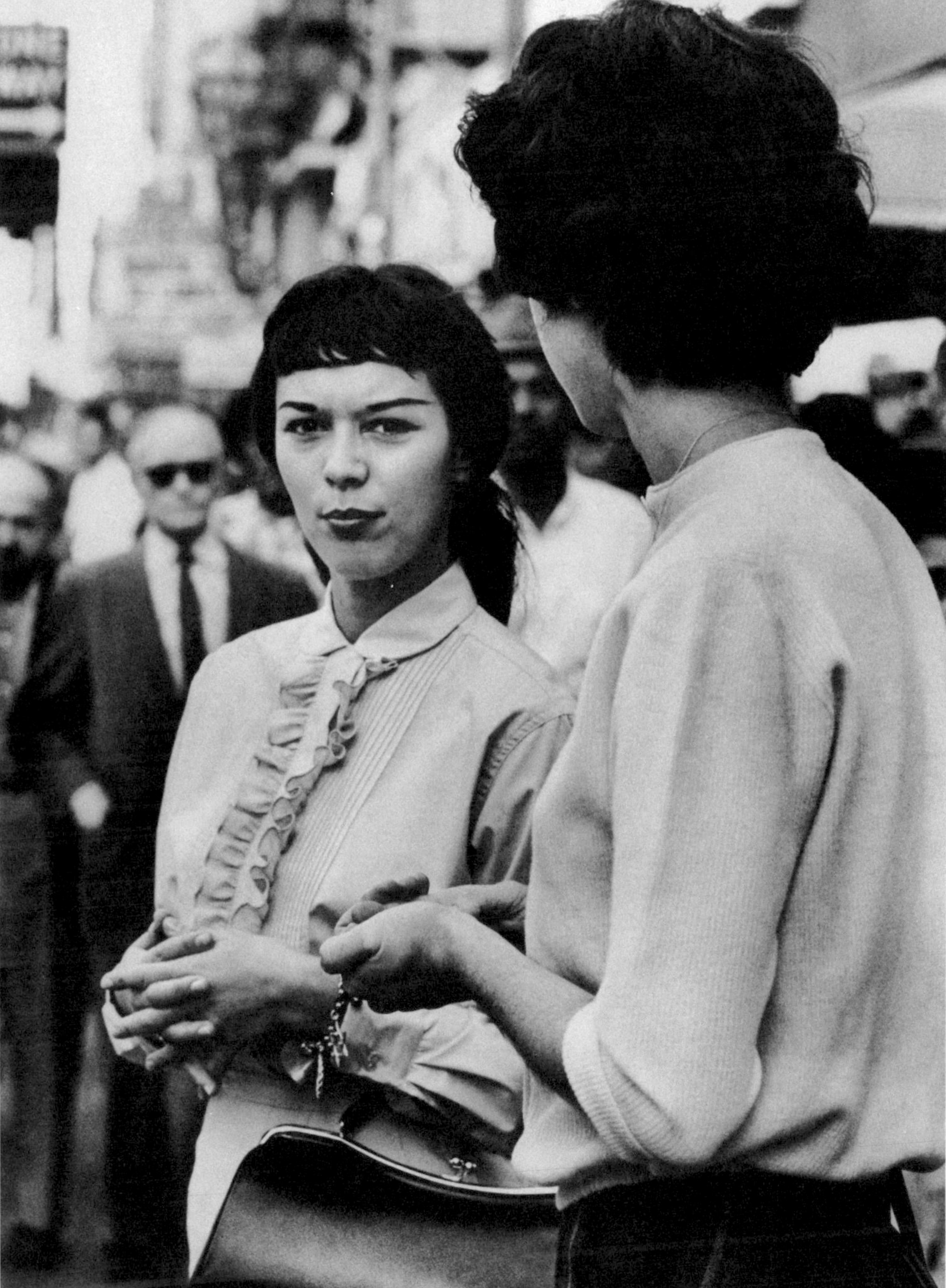

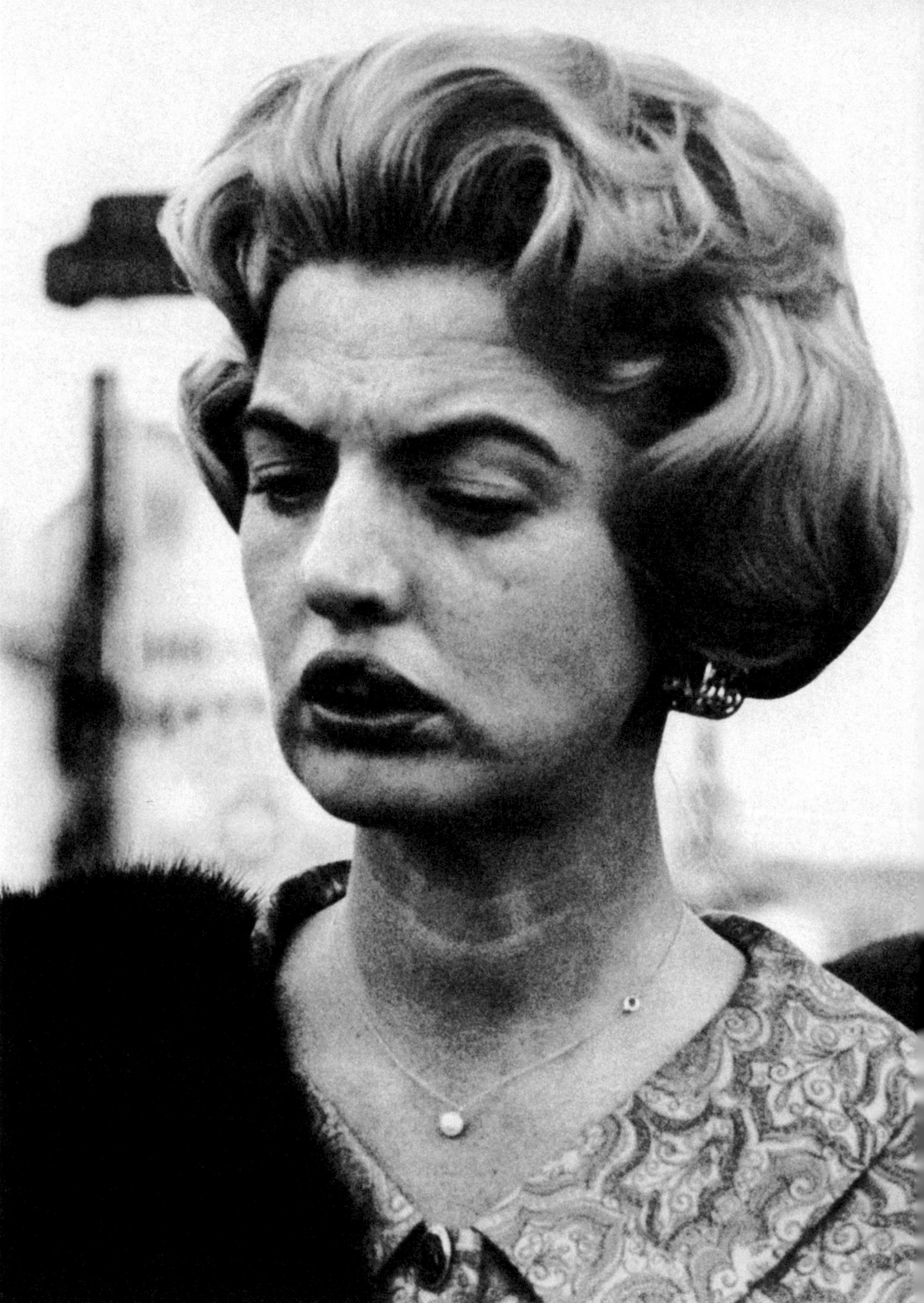

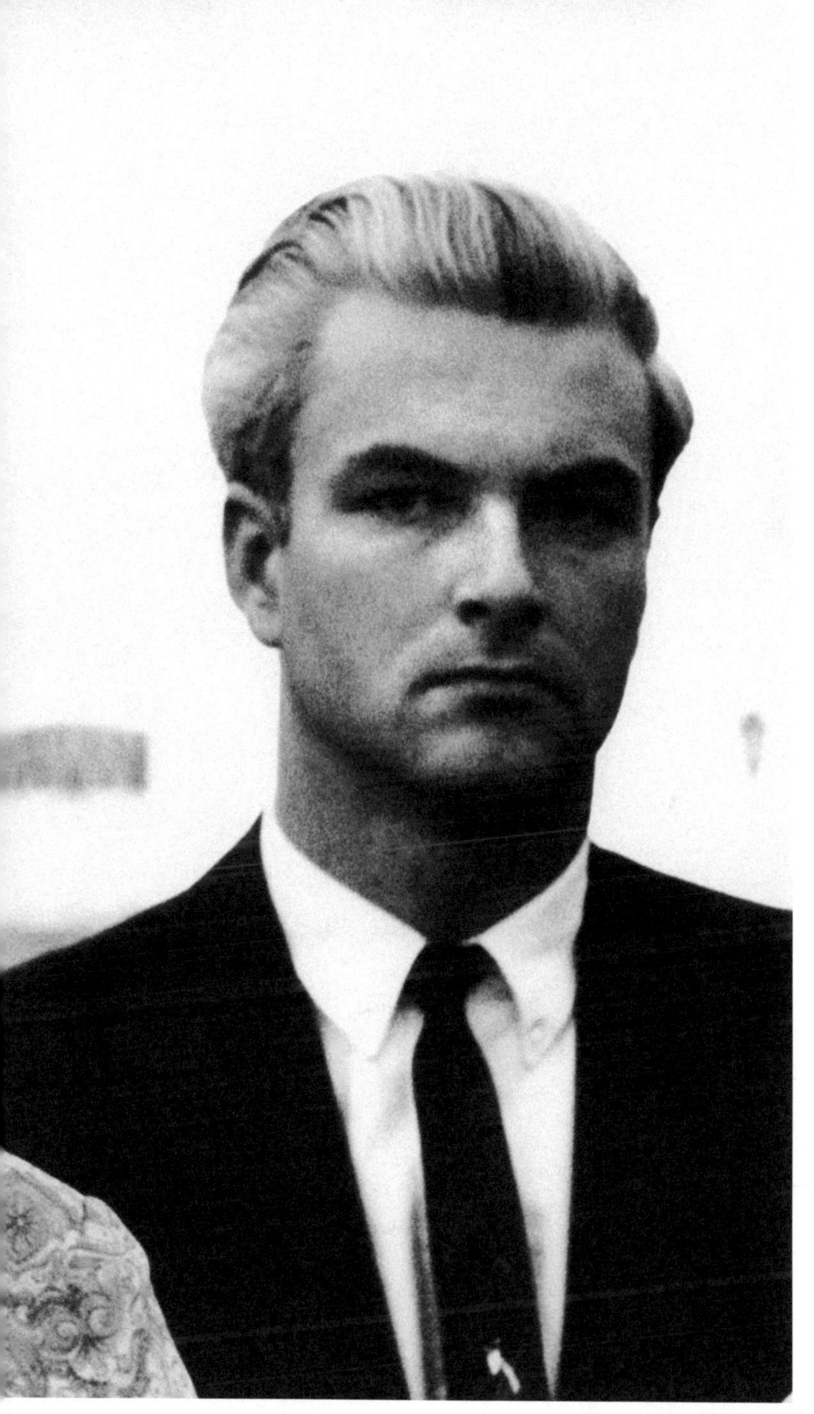

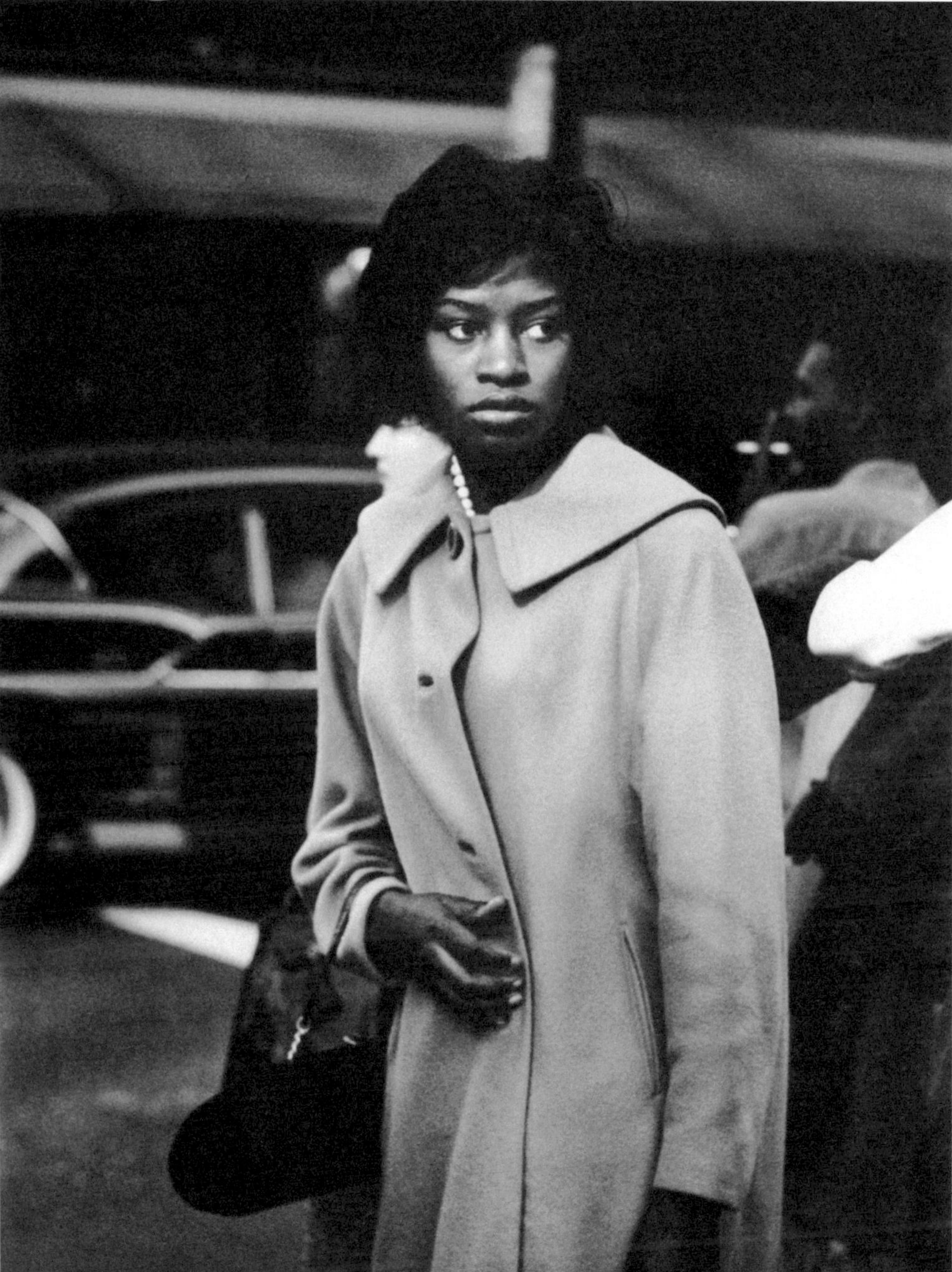

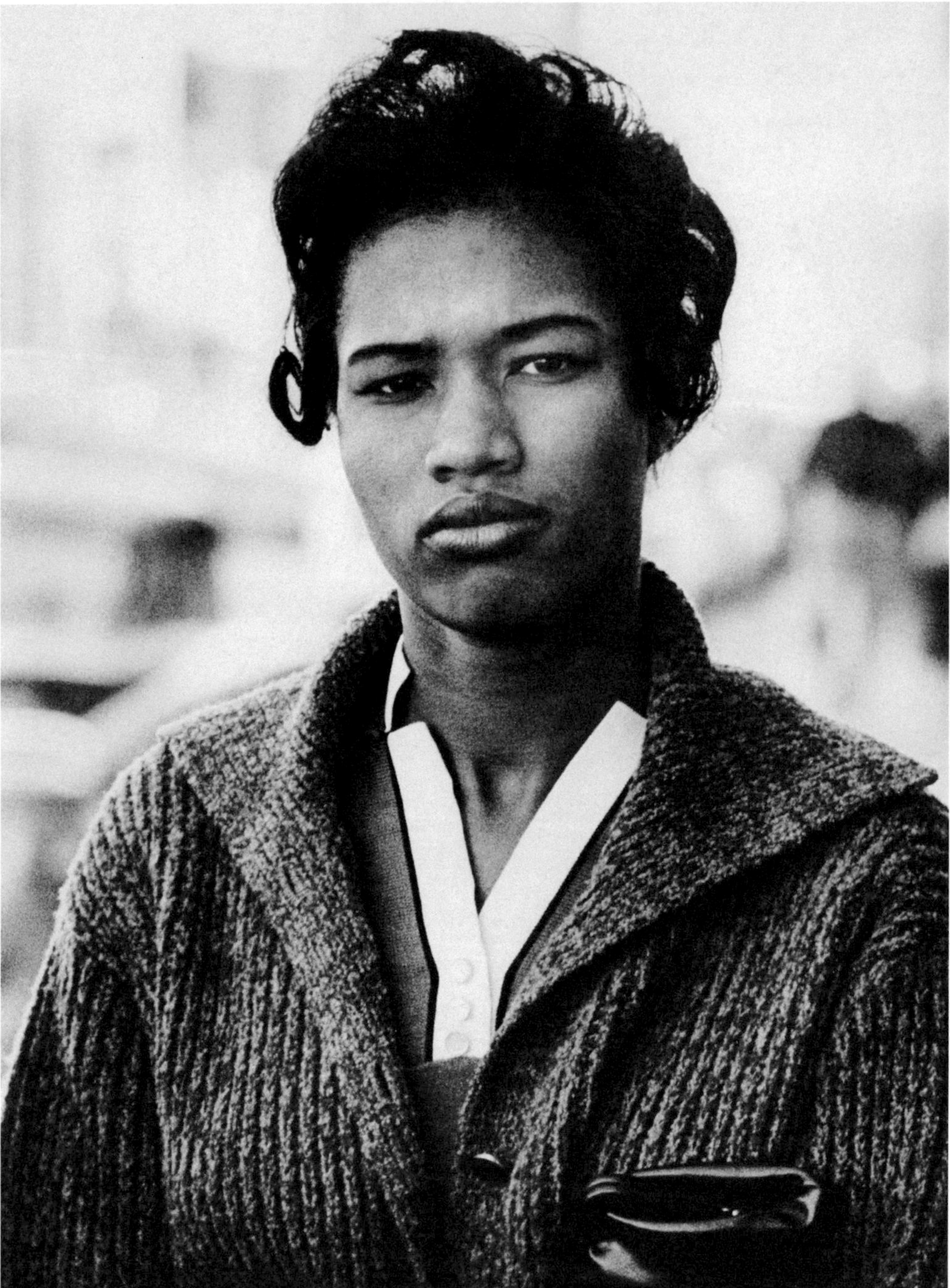

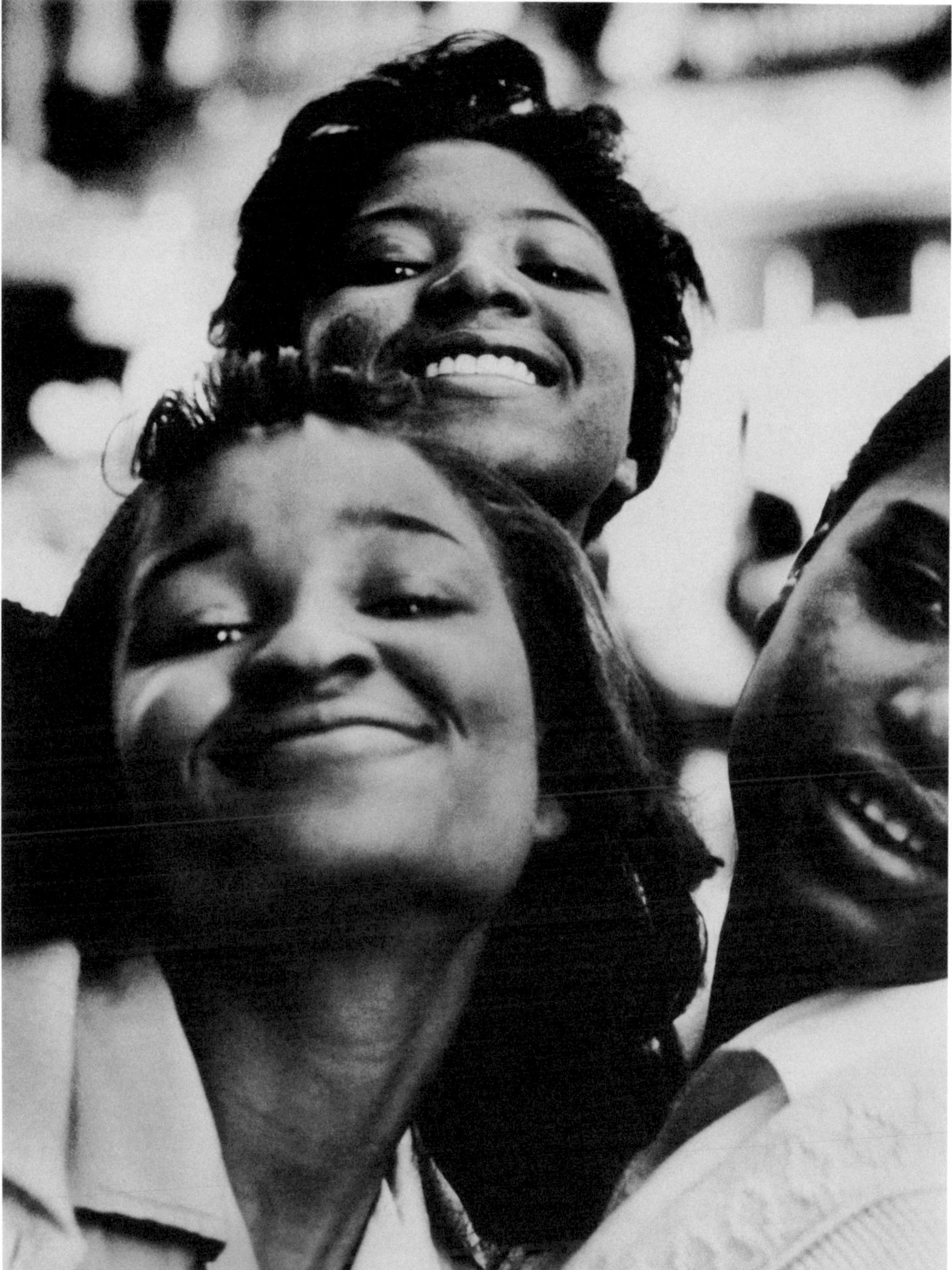

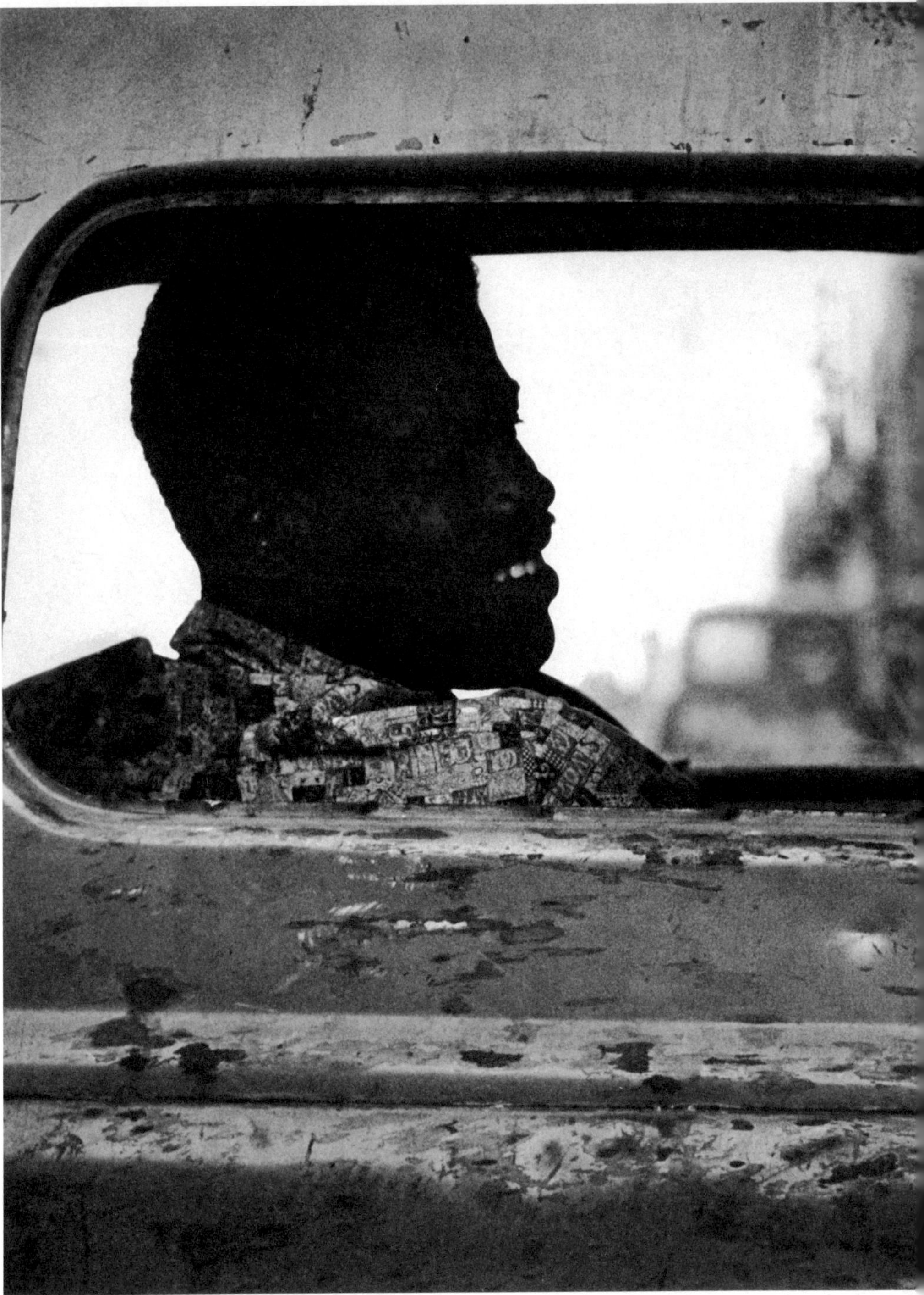

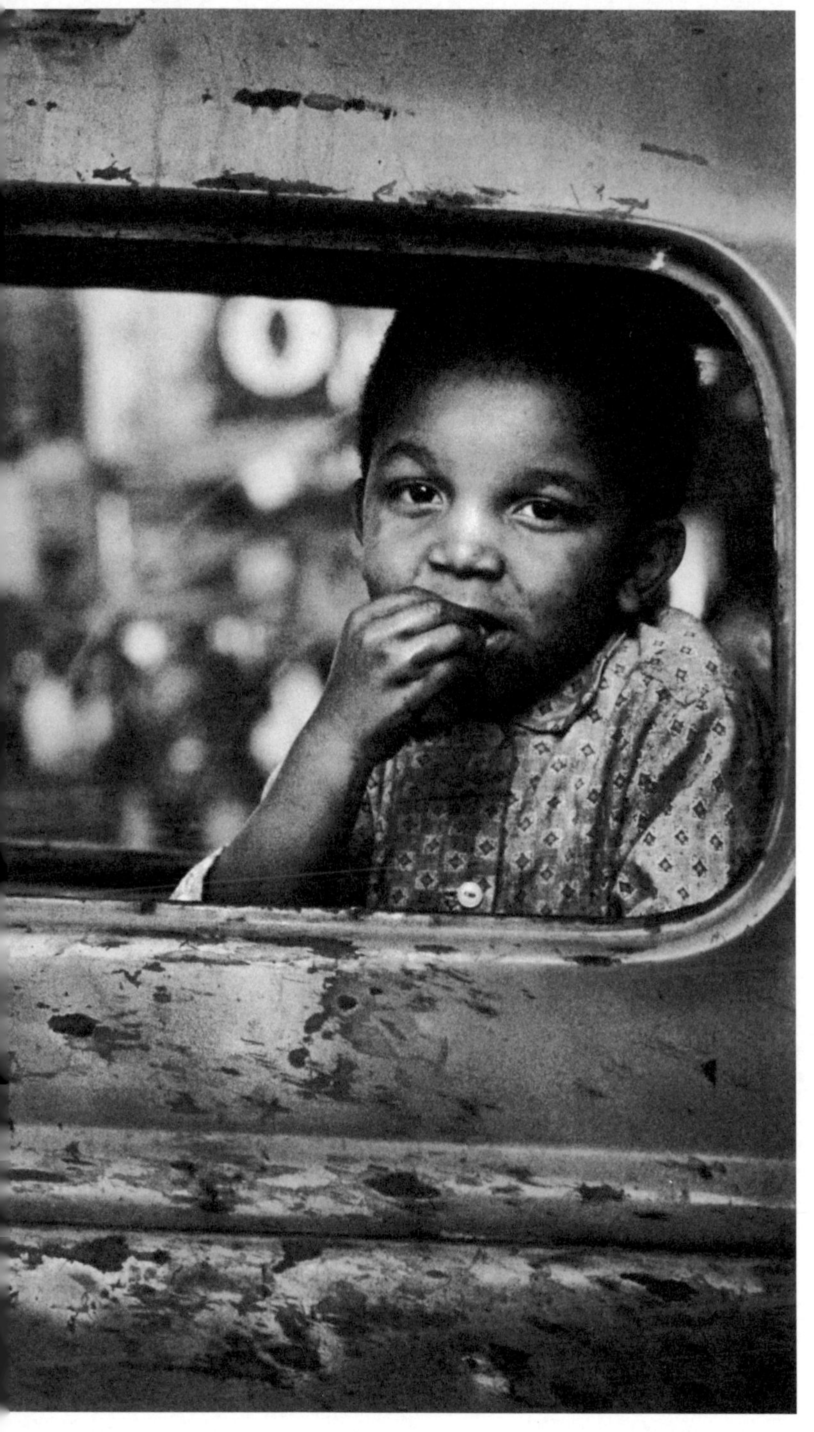

Printed in a first edition of 500 copies. Special edition of 50 copies, numbered, with print — numbered, signed and stamped by the Christer Strömholm Estate.

Published in Stockholm, Sweden by Libraryman, in cooperation with the Christer Strömholm Estate | Joakim Strömholm and Jakob Strömholm. Research by Anna Nilsdotter. Printed in Mölnlycke, Sweden by By Wind. Edited and designed in Paris, France by Tony Cederteg.

The photographs were taken in Los Angeles, 1963 and in New York, 1965.

ISBN : 978-91-88113-76-4

libraryman.se
stromholm.com

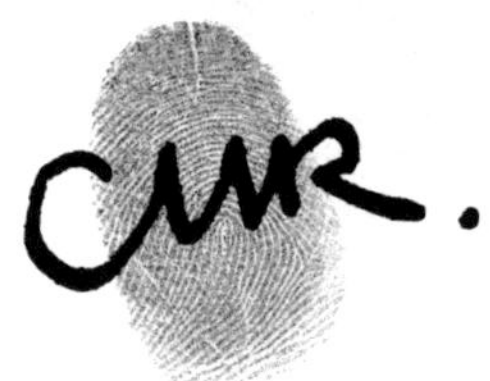

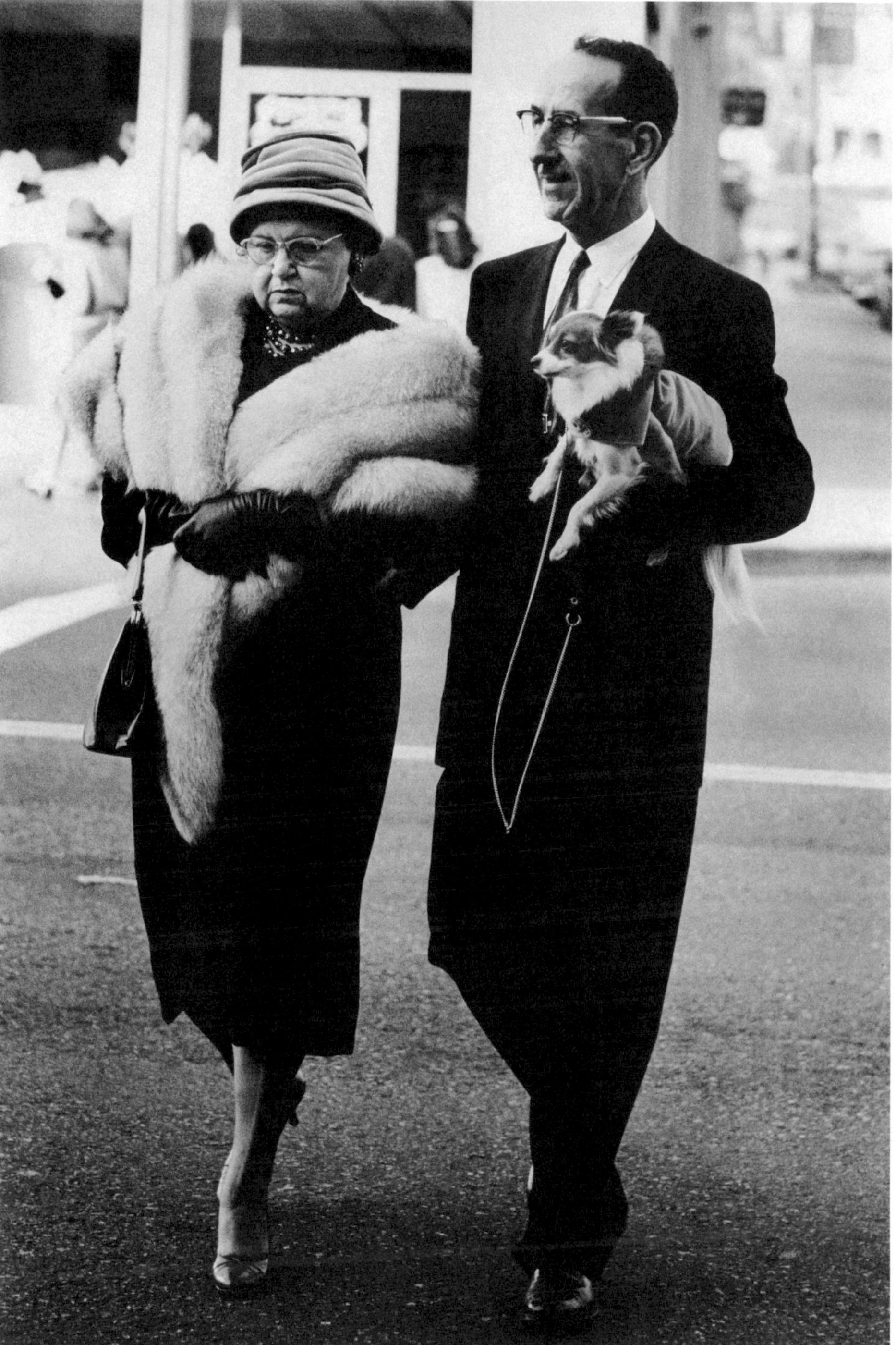

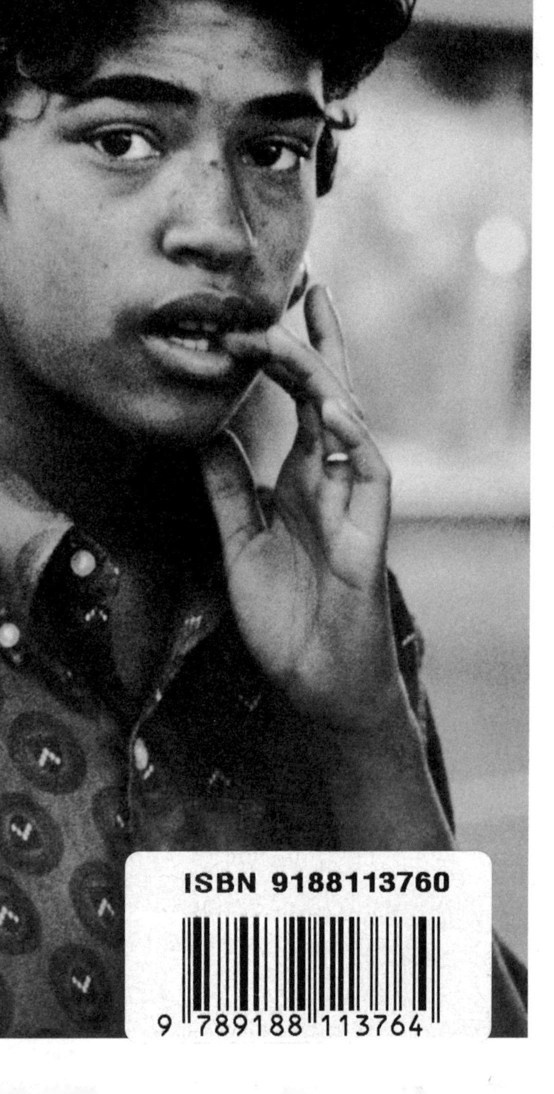

Christer Strömholm Unseen : United States of America

ISBN 9188113760

9 789188 113764